PASSPORT READY

ELEVATING THE LEVEL OF EXPECTATION IN SELF AND LESSER IN OTHERS

STEVEN J. CALDWELL

authorHOUSE®

AuthorHouse™
1663 Liberty Drive
Bloomington, IN 47403
www.authorhouse.com
Phone: 1 (800) 839-8640

Published by AuthorHouse 12/17/2018

ISBN: 978-1-5462-7129-1 (sc)
ISBN: 978-1-5462-7127-7 (hc)
ISBN: 978-1-5462-7128-4 (e)

Library of Congress Control Number: 2018914391

Print information available on the last page.

Contents

Contents

Introduction

While visiting the pristine waters and luscious landscape of Jamaica, I was asked upon leaving did I have my passport? I told my wife it was in the safe. She went to retrieve it and asked the question, can I see where you have been, I said certainly you may. As she perused my passport she noticed that I had been to Mexico and then responded, "I didn't know you'd been to Mexico." I said yes, that's the reason I got the passport in the first place. While flying back to Miami, I began to think about the question, I didn't know you'd been to Mexico? That question kept repeating in my mind and then it hit me. You see I served as team chaplain and life coach for the University of Miami, football, women's basketball, soccer and track for 20 years. In the summer of 2007 Coach Katie Meier had asked me to accompany the team to Mexico for possibly two weeks. I told her that I'd love to go, she said great ... do you have your passport? I didn't, so I had to apply for it. I thought about that deeply on the plane. I pondered, what if the trip to Cancun, Mexico was sooner than it took for me to get my passport. If the time it took to obtain it was longer than the schedule trip, then the team would've gone without me and I would've missed an opportunity to experience an all expenses paid trip to one of the worlds most beautiful place. I would have missed my moment. The door that was open to me would have been squandered because I was not Passport Ready. I was living my life without any expectation to ever go outside the United States. I was not expecting to go anywhere, to experience anything than what I was used to and what I knew. I wondered how many people in the world are like I was? Waking up everyday existing but not living. No vision, no plan, and no purpose! How many people are not Passport Ready, when the time comes for them get what they have been waiting for only to find out they are not ready for what's been waiting for them. The door of opportunity would've been shut, and the next level life lessons would have been missed. So, are you living life not being passport ready? Do you find that you are existing in the world and not living? Do you need help in figuring out what you need to do to get ready for your open-door experience, well this book is for you! It doesn't matter where you came from, where you're at in life, what only matters is where you're going.

My story is a message of highs and deep lows. I was born and raised on the southside of Chicago. My secondary education was in an urban setting, I am a proud graduate of Chicago Vocational High School better know as (CVS). I was a very good baseball player, an all-star in fact, playing for the highly esteem Jackie Robinson West summer baseball league. I had a lot going for me in high school. I felt that baseball would be my ticket out of the inner city and on my way to stardom, but the bottom dropped out and the rug of baseball stardom was pulled from underneath me. It happened while playing for a traveling all-star team in New York. It was there that I believed that I could celebrate me winning the MVP of the tournament with smoking weed. When I started smoking was the day when I lost my vison for what was ahead of me, I was trapped in the present … in the now. Many stellar athletes must be reminded of being expendable. As team chaplain for the University of Miami Football program which I served for 20 years, I often had to remind these men of this word. You must employ advanced decision-making techniques into your life, because every now decision affects your future position in life. You must make decisions in your present that will position you in a positive place in your future.

I didn't think like that as a young man and I had no one helping me to make decisions. I only had coaches on the field but no one to coach me through life. So, I made my decisions based on my circumstances and I believed the hype about who people said I was, but that light soon dimmed in to darkness.

My life spiraled out of control, drugs took over and I no longer saw myself as someone who had a meaningful future. I know this because of the decisions I was making. I lost my baseball scholarship at Florida Memorial University (Miami, FL), this lead me to becoming a squatter because I had to move out of the dorms, no longer did I have the financial aid to supply that need. I was living in a house in the Miami Gardens area of Dade County with no running water, no bed, no furniture but thank God I had the lights working. I started to sell cocaine for a local drug dealer and soon everything that I said I would not do … I was doing. However, I had as my momma would say, "A but God" moment. He stepped in.

Many people will argue about what truth is. Some, say truth is relative, others will argue that truth is absolute, but I want to argue another form of truth and that is experiential truth. It is what a person experiences in life. No one can tell you that what you experienced in life was not real to you and therefore, its truth to you. Well this was my experience. I and my fraternity brother were on our way to purchase drugs from a new dealer. We arrived and was told that we had to come back because the package was not ready. We went to the gas station and got some beer and while driving back to the house I heard a voice telling me to get out of the car. I hadn't smoked anything at this point only a swallow of Old English 800 and I am hearing voices? I ignored the voice and again with greater forced I heard it … GET OUT THE CAR! I told my frat brother to stop the car because he hadn't heard what I was hearing. I told him I had to get out and that I couldn't go with him. He had a few choice words for me and left me standing on the corner of 62nd street and 12th ave in the heart of the city which is called the pork and beans (the first 48). Well, my frat came running down the street ten minutes later, when he got to me blood was flowing from his head, he said they had robbed him stole my car and the $5000.00 we had to purchase the drugs. He was grazed in the head from a gunshot. It was that day the helped transform my life. I asked God to lead me and I promised Him that I would follow. Things haven't been all milk and honey for me since that day, but my life has turned out to be an incredible journey. The one thing I have come to realize is, as much as I want life to be a bed of roses, I must realize that every beautiful rose has its thrones.

As I look back over my life I can see how I would've made better decisions if I was Passport Ready. If I had expectations to go some where and be someone. To become a value added individual and a transformational leader. I never saw that about me, but God did, and I hope you let my story and experience help you make better decisions in your life and elevate your thinking about who you are and where you're going.

I want to walk you through what it takes to have vision for your life. Why and how you need to change how you see yourself in this world and to know it doesn't matter where you came from you can live your best life. I will attempt to instill in you the cognitive awareness of your surroundings and help you make a shift upwards in your thinking and your seeing. So, if you are ready to go on this journey of being empowered, inspired, encouraged, energized, equipped and elevated then this book is for you, it's your time to walk through your open door of opportunity … don't want you to miss it, so let's Go!

Chapter 1

Living Life without Expectation

William Shakespeare said,

> I always feel happy, You know why?
> Because I don't expect anything from anyone.
> Expectations always hurt. Life is short, so love your
> life.
> Be happy and keep smiling. Just live for yourself
> And before your speak, Listen. Before your write,
> Think.
> Before you spend, Earn. Before you pray, Forgive.
> Before you hurt, Feel. Before you hate, Love.
> Before you quit, Try. Before you die, Live.

Shakespeare has an interesting philosophy here. He wants us to believe we should go through life without expectations. But his philosophical expression is a half-truth. Here he states he doesn't have expectations regarding people, but that doesn't mean he was living life without any expectations.

What is an expectation? It is a strong belief that something will happen. Synonyms for *expectation* are words like *prospect*, *potential*, *outlook*, and *hope*. So for William

Shakespeare to say, as some have syllogized, who do not live life with expectation is a false assumption. Rather, the main point that I have deduced from his view on expectation is to not have it in other people so much that you forfeit your happiness. Rather, have more expectations of oneself, including expecting to live a happy life. I mean, how can one live a happy life without expecting to do so? I agree that to have unrealistic expectations in people is what brings hurt and disappointment. Many people have what I call the three selves—false self, actual self, and true self. I briefly introduce these concepts here and I will expand on them later.

The false self is in my estimation, 80% of the time; it is this false self we want others to believe. The actual self is the self we know but don't want others to discover. And the true self is the one waiting for us to recognize who we are and why we were created. So to live life in falsity is certainly what Shakespeare was referring to when he said having expectations in people only leads to hurt and disappointment.

On this I would agree. But what about your life? Will you be imprisoned with the false assumption not to have expectations? If so, the person you'll be hurting the most is you! You must have expectations in life. If you don't, I would venture to say you have yet to live, to experience your best life. To live life without expectations is not living at all; you are merely existing, existing in the now with no plan or focus on your future. One of the most challenging things in life is to meet the challenge of life. What am I referring to?

Well, life will challenge you, and when it does, you have to determine your response. Being reactionary to life and its challenges causes you to make emotional decisions rather than thoughtful ones. I tell my football players and other student athletes a truth that has helped me tremendously: it is not what happens to you that matters, but it is how you respond to what happens that matters.

I have made some emotional decisions in my life that still affect me, but I have made up my mind that I am a winner. It doesn't matter how far I fall; I expect to bounce back. I love Proverbs 24:16. It reads from the Berean Study Bible, "For though a righteous man falls seven times, he will get up, but the wicked stumble in times of calamity." What a powerful verse! Look at the oxymoronic aspect of this verse, "righteous falling." You would think that surely righteous men or women would never fall, because they are right people, hence righteous. But *righteous* doesn't mean perfect. It means you have a sense of morality; you have value and are virtuous. But it never meant perfect. This is what Shakespeare was referring to, I believe. We look for the perfect in the imperfect and are disappointed every time. But how we respond when this happens is what helps us elevate our thinking and harness our emotions and reactions. If you see yourself as a winner, you will respond as one in times of calamity. You must expect to bounce back from whatever life hits you with. This verse gives me strength and is empowering.

In my opinion, one of the greatness strengths is that of transparency. We do not like to be transparent. Not being transparent keeps us covered and protected from the mean individuals of life. You must expect that. You must want to be free from people taking your power to be transparent.

I suffered from depression. However, I convince myself every day that I am a winner. Do I have to fight to maintain that mind-set? Damn right I do. I lean on the positive clarification of God's Word about who I am. I remind myself of the things I have already overcome and how He has brought me through. I surround myself with a team of influencers who help to keep me moving forward toward the prize. I challenge myself to rethink me and expect greater of myself each day. I remind myself that I am a "more than."

You may wonder, *What is a more than?* I am happy to tell you. Some see themselves as conquerors, but I see myself as more than a conqueror. It's the more than that keeps me moving, not the mentality of a conqueror. Paul says in Roman 8:37, "Nay, in all these things we are more than conquerors through Him who loved us." So that means you are more than your heartache, more than your pain, more than your disappointments, more than your hiccups and bad habits, more than your setbacks? Yes, you are, but you must believe that you are what you think and believe you are. You must expect to be someone and do something in your life that only you can do. This is the call, the purpose. If you are breathing right now, you are pregnant with purpose. Don't let life challenge you so much that you lose sight of your purpose, or if you have yet to discover your purpose you need to know that the journey of discovering it is a joy.

Live your life with expectation to be, for Shakespeare said, "To be or not to Be that is the question." Are you going to be, or are you not going to expect to be somebody and go somewhere significant?

Remember, I didn't have my passport for the Mexico trip because I didn't expect to ever go outside the continental United States. I couldn't see that for myself, so I lived life with no expectation. The blessing is that I was given time. Time to change my mind-set and do the work to go beyond what I saw for myself. I had time to fill out the application, I had time to go through the process, and when the process was done, what I never thought I would experience began to happen.

But what if I didn't have the time? I would have missed my open-door opportunity. I would not have experienced all the culture and comradery of being with those I loved and was helping to lead. I would have missed a blessing because I never saw in myself what others had seen. I had to change my thinking and my expectation of me. I became passport ready!

How have you thought about yourself?

Do you see yourself making changes?

When do you expect to start your process of change, and what are your expectations?

Chapter 2

Where I Am, I Am Not Always Going to Be (Advanced decision)

In 1995, I was a successful youth pastor of what we would call a megachurch today. I was involved in the lives of all the youth in our church. I was pastoring about five hundred or so youth between the ages of thirteen and eighteen, and God was really blessing us.

I was single and looking for a wife to be by my side because being a handsome young man in full-time ministry was so hard. (There's that transparency again.) But it was. I had difficult days and some not so difficult ones as I navigated the treacherous waters of being single and in ministry. I had my eye on this beautiful sister at the church. She was easy on the optic nerve, anatomically correct, and morphologically sound; she was fine and beautiful! We went out a few times, but she didn't see me the way I saw her. But I would always tell her, "You are a pastor's wife." She would respond, "That's not for me." I kept telling her, but she thought I was trying to manipulate her into thinking that she was.

She told me she was the wife of a professional ball player. She had expectations of being on the *Real Housewives* franchise. I told her she must give me a chance because I felt she was the type of woman I wanted and needed to keep my attention.

As it turns out, she chose another man to date, and as they say, the rest is history. I ran into her fifteen years later, and to my surprise, she was a preacher's wife but not the pastor's wife I saw her to be for me. When we saw each other, she could hardly speak. We exchanged pleasantries as she introduced me to her husband. She had heard about what God had done for me. How I was a successful senior pastor at the New Providence Missionary Baptist Church in Miami. How I was the team chaplain of the University of Miami and that I traveled with the team that won a national championship of arguably the best college football team in history. She had heard how I was a professor of religion and philosophy at Florida Memorial University. She had heard that I was the Congress of Christian Education president for the Seaboard Baptist Association and how I mentored and was the life coach to several NFL players. In other words, she'd heard that I was a successful man. She was a very successful educator and administrator in her own right.

As we caught up with each other I felt compelled to ask her, what about me made her go in a different direction? You know us men, I had to find out what I did, her reply to me was, "You said I was going to marry a preacher." I responded with, no I didn't, I said you were supposed to be a pastor's wife and you were to be my wife. I took the bold step and asked her why didn't she give me the chance? She replied, "I didn't see you the way you are today, all I saw then was a youth pastor and didn't think of what you could or would be." Wow, what a revelation! She gave up on me because she thought that where I was I was always going to be. Sadly, my story is replicated in more than enough lives to count, but the difference is, I didn't not have the expectations of myself as she had of me. My friend never allow what others think of you to become your reality, rather move beyond the perception of others into the reality of self. Self-awareness, self-care, self-love and self-actualization. Now this self-actualization I would venture to say is a bit more philosophical than it is psychological. It is more than what Abraham Maslow suggest in his hierarchy of needs. I am not suggesting that one grow toward the fulfillment of the highest needs, nor am I suggesting as Carl Rogers theory of growth potential of the the real self and the ideal self, rather I am suggesting that you look at who you really are mainly, your flaws and inabilities and learn to cultivate a life based on these factors. I wanted to be what I have become and becoming. I knew that I wasn't the most talented nor the most gifted preacher, pastor, professor or chaplain but I did know I was unique. I didn't look at my unique skill set as something to be frowned upon but rather embraced. I realized how God had wired me differently and that to fit inside the cookie jar was not my calling, I was not an assimilator but and innovator. Mother always said, "Its not what people call you, it's what you answer too." I refuse to let others tell me what I can't do. As a matter of fact, it fuels me when people try to place limits on my life, especially when I serve a God of no limitations!

When I asked people how's it going, and they respond withy, I'm just going with the flow. That would be a nice casual response, but I think differently. I follow up with an interrogative question, do you know where the flow is going? I mean that's like getting in a car with others to just joy ride and to find out that your joy ride lands you unconscious in the hospital. You can't just joy ride through life, you need to be intentional about your life, to just go with the flow is like man looking in a mirror and forgetting what he looks like after he has left his image.

So, where are you now? What does your present circumstance say to you about where you want to go and who you want to become? Do you see yourself as someone who will always be what you are and where you are the rest of your life, or can you get your passport ready to experience transformation? Are you overly concern with what others say about you? Well let me help you. It doesn't matter what they think just don't allow negative thoughts from others become your reality. As I refer to the young lady at the beginning of this chapter I had to wonder if her present life was something that she saw. She couldn't see me in the future and now in my mind I wonder if she looks back at our past thinking about her and my present; thinking about how our future are would have been if she could've only believe in my potential and embraced the future me in our past. The point I'm making is, just because she couldn't see it didn't t mean I had to stop looking for it. I was on my way somewhere, but where life would take me would blow my mind. I didn't see me taking young men and helping them develop into NFL stars. Stars like Ed Reed, Reggie Wayne, Santana Moss, Edrrine James, Andre Johnson, Clinton Portis, Vernon Carey, Vince Wilfork, Willis McGehee, Frank Gore, Jarred Payton, David Njoku, Duke Johnson, Michael Jackson and so many more. I had the opportunity to be apart of a national championship team and to meet countless celebrities because of it. Never in my dreams did I see this, but I did know that God was taking me somewhere but never realized just how special my somewhere would be!

It is said that the journey of a 1000 miles begins with one step. I would suggest that the first step is to have greater expectation for one's self. You may find yourself in a setting of a group of great people. You'll look around and see all of the greats, but there is another person that you have failed to see … you! You can be sitting with the great, amongst the great and not realize that you have a seat at the table. Do not belittle your moment. You may look at yourself and think that its not your time. You're not ready, but I am here to tell you that when ever you think its not your turn it will be your time.

I was standing in line at Walmart. You know how they have the staggered checkout lines. Well I was the eighth person in the line. While waiting a young lady came up and opened a new checkout right next to the line I was in. She looked at me as the I was the last person in line, after while I was in and said these beautiful words to me, Sir, can I help you? I quickly moved in her direction, paid for my things and walked out looking at everyone that was in line ahead of me previously and just smiled and walked out happy. When I got in my car I heard in my Spirit ... what did you just experience and what did learn. I didn't even think that I was having a teachable moment while in Walmart. Well the light turned on and I said God I got it, It was not my turn but it was my time. It was my time which made it my turn. I was the eighth person in line, clearly it was not my turn, however I was in the right place being in eighth place, even though it was not my turn it was my time! When you live life with the expectation of being somebody and going somewhere, it will seem as though you will never get your chance. Keep believing that you are next even when all the circumstances say different. You may be last in line but that doesn't mean anything with God. The first shall be last and the last shall be first. God has the power to change you life! Stay on the path of somewhere even when it looks like its going nowhere ... because it may not be your turn but it will be your time. Be Passport Ready when your time comes. Don't hesitate at the opportunity. Walk through that door of favor, you are Passport Ready!

Chapter 3

Paradigm Shift …
(You can't stay here!)

It has been said that familiarity breeds contempt. That I believe is a true statement. However, I believe that familiarity breeds contentment. A synonym for this word is satisfaction. You have become a settler in your level of life and you're not trying to do anything more, but what if there is more out there waiting for you? Have you decided that you have arrived? Well my friend if you have made that decision then your life has just ended. You have declared that you have completed your life's journey and purpose, but here's the caveat, why do you still wake up in the morning? You wake because God still has something for you to do. You have a life to change, a person to help, a love to ignite you have greater things to do and the enemy to that is being content with where you are, but I' m to tell you that you don't have time to stay there because you now have somewhere else to go.

In Paradigm Pioneers, futurist Joel Barker shows that in the 21st century, settlers will be at the highest risk. When the followers call out: "Is it safe out there?", the pioneers will answer: "Sure but there's nothing left for you!"

Business used to be like the old west. After the pioneers blazed new trails, settlers behind them would call out: "Is it safe yet?" When the pioneers called back: "Yes, it's safe now.", the settlers would follow, benefiting from the pioneers risk-taking.

Joel Barker is sending forth a challenge. In his book he looks at two different paradigms. One is that of a settler and that of a pioneer. What's the difference? Pioneers don't become content, while settler do what they do … settle.

What is a paradigm? In layman term it is the way you see the world and you in it. Where do you fit in this big world? With all the people in this world what's so special about you? Can you truly be a significant person or are you seeing yourself as just the average Joe, just and ordinary person? Well if you are a settler then this is what you believe. I want you to not settle for being ordinary, but be extraordinary. In the movie Dead Poets Society, Robin Williams plays a professor of literature at a boarding school. One of the greatest lines in that movie is when he whispers those two great Latin terms … Carpe Diem … Seize the Day, make your lives extraordinary.

Listen to those words … make your life extraordinary. You have a choice. What do you want to do with your life? Do you want to be mediocre or do you want to be magnificent? Those who are mediocre are delusional in their thinking. They like for people to believe that they are pioneers but they really are nothing but settlers. Mediocre people love to give the testimony of climbing the mountain but they don't tell you they only made it half way up because the climb became too difficult. They want you to think they completed the climb but in reality they didn't. You have to shift your vision. I love what God says to Jeremiah in chapter 29:11, I know the thoughts that I think towards you says The Lord, thoughts of good and not of evil, to give you a future and a hope. Wow if God can think that way about Jeremiah, I know He can think that way about me, so I embraced that thought, I remind myself that God thinks highly of me and has declared He as a plan for my future. I cannot settle, I have to keep pushing myself toward my dreams and goals. I can't allow negative images to become my reality. I have to believe that there is something greater for me and I know its waiting for my arrival. However, I will not arrive there if I can't see myself being there. I need to shift my vison, shift my focus and live what I see. The question is, do you know your value and how do you value yourself?

When Lebron James was coming out of High School into the NBA, his current living conditions where very meager. His mother lived in subsidized housing paying only 17 dollars a month for rent. Reebok an athletic apparel company offered him a shoe deal for 10 million dollars. What a come up right? However, Lebron did not take the deal. You mean he had nothing and they offered 10 million dollars and he didn't take it? Lebron says that he didn't take it because he knew what he was worth. A few weeks later Nike came along and offered him a 90 million dollar contract, that deal later turned into a lifetime contract of 1billion dollars.

Know your worth! Lebron did, Know that you have value and don't settle because others may want you to. In business there is a characterization expressed as value added. You must see yourself as an value added individual. Shift your paradigm and believe in who God created you to be and don't settle for being mediocre ... Carpe Diem!

> *When you change the way you look at things, the things you look at CHANGE!*
>
> `Wayne Dyer

Chapter Four

Travel Plans
(True self, false self actual self)

Wow, you've decided to make a change. If you've made it to chapter four, you have been challenged to expect more of yourself and less in others. You have begun to sense that you are ready for your next level. You can see a different you in your future and you have learned not to settle but to pioneer. Well what's next? It's time to plan your trip. Trip … what trip you may be asking. Yeah you're thinking that this book is about changing and challenging your expectations, well it is, but after you have begun the shift you have to plan your journey to your place of purpose, destiny and fulfillment. Plan to take your Passport with you … let's go!

You are getting excited about your trip to Vegas, its your first time and man you are on the seat of your pants waiting for the date to come. Finally the date that you have chosen to go is here but wait, you didn't purchase your plane ticket, you forgot to get the hotel reserved and the rental car. There was never an itinerary for your trip and you didn't even shop for that new outfit for the trip. Better yet, you didn't pack a thing for the trip you were just too excited about the date you chose, that you didn't plan your trip! I know this sounds absurd however, it is how many people think when it comes to planning their lives. They are excited about what they are going to do that they never do it. It is said that if you don't plan for success you arbitrarily plan for failure. It doesn't take much effort in planning to fail but it does take a lot in planning to succeed.

Ok, so you know that you're going somewhere and where you are you're not staying but how do you get to where you know you're going? Well let me suggest to you a few steps in making your travel plans.

First, research where you're going. Look at what that place offers you and what you can bring to it. Find out what that place of purpose is in need of that you can provide. Develop your goals and objectives. Build your itinerary for personal development and then position yourself.

Secondly, Speak to those that have done what you want to do or been where you are trying to go. They may have been there before you but they are not you. You bring your own unique set of skills to the place of purpose. Never lose sight of this, you are unique, some may have similarities but they are not you. Mind map with them and mine for new concepts and ideas while speaking to them. Glean and ask questions, never stop asking questions. The more questions you can come up with the more information you attain. Never, never, never get tired of asking question no matter how insignificant it may seem to you it may be a question that never had been asked before.

Thirdly, plan for detours. Sometimes when you are traveling you may encounter delays or even cancellations. Remember these are nothing but detours and sometimes being rerouted may occur. Remember its not what happens to you that matters but what … how you respond. Be prepared for detours. You may have a project not develop as you saw it but that doesn't mean it will not be completed. This is where your contingency plan kicks in. This is why you asked all those questions because you need to have a back up plan in place. Also, plan for people to let you down during this process. You may be thinking how pessimistic can I be telling you this, well you will be working with people that can't see what you see and for that reason alone they will abort the plan but don't sweat it, you already planned for their departure.

Fourthly, employ people with one singular purpose and that is to get you where you need to be. You can't do it alone, its to big for just you, you have to have some help to get to the finish line. Your goal is to complete the race not just start the race. Find the experts that can help you build what you see. There are those that possess what you do not.

One of the greatest coaches in NBA history is Hall of Fame coach Phil Jackson. He is one of the most winningest coaches in NBA history but Phil Jackson understood his limitations and inabilities. He hired a offensive guru by the name of Tex Winters. We don't hear much about Tex and if you ask Phil Jackson what contributed to his success as a coach, he would say Tex Winters. Without the offensive mind of Tex Winters Phil Jackson wouldn't have won as many games or championships that he did. Phil Jackson planned to win but knew his limitation was offensive coaching … he left that to Tex Winters the architect of the triangle offense. 11 NBA championships later both men are in the NBA Hall of Fame.

Your Hall of Fame awaits you. Plan your route. Chose where you want to go. Talk with those who have the experience what you are searching for. Have a contingency plan in place but don't let the detour stop you. Sometimes they are divine interruptions that enhance your ability to succeed in your place of purpose. Failure is a part of the process, no inventor got it right the first time but they kept at it until the idea worked, don't give up when you've been detoured. Lastly, know your limitations and employ someone specifically to do what you are limited at doing. Winning is success! When you learn how to win you will experience success. It takes preparation (mental focus), planning (cognitive awareness) and performance (physical exertion), remember that it will not be easy but it will be worth it. There are going to be those days when you get knocked down but you have to find that get back up in you. It was Ford Motors that had a slogan a while back, it said that Ford trucks were built to last. I took that slogan, expanded it and personalized it … Steven J. Caldwell not just built to last but built to outlast. I have determined that I will fight for what I want and for who I believe in. When you plan your trip remember to pack your core values. These are the essentials to staying the course. As you move through the maze of discovering your purpose and destiny, you will be asked to be uncomfortable, and not just once but several times. If you employ advanced decision making techniques you will win. Every decision you make today has an effect on your tomorrow. It is a true statement, better decisions better outcome, bad decision horrible outcome. Choose wisely what you want to do and how you want to get there but know this … you can't take everyone with you.

> *"A goal without a plan is just a wish."*

> — Antoine de Saint-Exupéry

Chapter Five

Passing through Customs
(You can't take everyone with you)

As your overseas adventure draws to a close and you travel home, you will be asked to fill out a customs declaration form, the first step in completing your Customs and Border Protection passport inspection and interview with a customs officer. (If you are driving across an international border, you will not be asked to fill out the form, but you will have to tell a customs officer what you bought while you were out of the country.)

When you arrive at Passport Control or an international border, a Customs and Border Protection officer will review your declaration form, examine your passport and ask you about your trip and about the items you are bringing back with you.

If you plan ahead, you can help make the customs inspection process flow smoothly. (Trip Savvy 2016)
This excerpt is from an article in Trip Savvy, in it there are some very important items that should be paid close

attention to. One of those items is proper planning … plan ahead to make your process smooth.

This idea is from our previous chapter and it fits well here. You may not make it through customs smoothly if there is no plan. In this process you have to go through a series of steps to make it through customs and on to your destination. The first stage of this process is the Declaration Stage.

The declaration stage is when you have to state what you are carrying or better yet conveying as you go into your place of purpose, now the caveat is … you can't take everything with you.

When you declare it is imperative that you right down everything in your possession. It means you have to speak and declare on paper. What does this stage have to do with you passing customs … everything.

When you declare you are making a statement of reason, it is your syllogism as to why you are and what you have been called to do. It is here that you speak about what you possess.

What have you declared about your life? What have you declared about who you are? What have you declared about you unique gift and calling. I love what the Apostle Paul wrote in Romans 11:29, in it he says "For the gift and the calling of God are irrevocable." Did you here that? Every person alive God has given gifts to. You may be looking at yourself and asking what gift do I have? You have a gift from the giver and He made no mistake in giving you the gift, your job is to know and declare who you are and why your gifted.

In 2004, I had the privilege to be the pregame speaker for the San Diego Chargers as they prepared to play the Miami Dolphins. I was excited about the opportunity and I thank God for opening that door. A point of clarity, when you declare your gift and know you're gifted the bible teaches us that it is your gifted that will make room for you to be in the presence of the great, (Proverbs 18:16). As I arrived to the team hotel, I was pumped. I wanted to impact, impress and inspire those who would be present. Here I am a young team chaplain at the University of Miami speaking to the San Diego Chargers. I was not some mega church pastor. I hadn't begun to Senior Pastor yet, but I knew that was in my future. I wasn't on television as some guru with profound wisdom to elevate you to paly the game. I wasn't selling books and on the New York times best sellers list. No I was none of those things, but one thing I was … I was gifted and I knew it! I knew that I poses the tools to handle the job that was given me. I knew that all of the struggles in my life were for this very reason. I knew who I was and was ready to share what God had gifted me to share. I made a declaration about me to me and I would not let anything deter me from what I believed about me … you must believe in yourself and I did!

I began to speak to them about the importance of appreciation. Being thankful and humble. Being a man of purpose and not just a Sunday performance. I asked them this question, what did you do, to deserve to be so gifted?

Yes you train, yes you practice, yes you study your play book, but I can do all of that and I will never be LaDamien Tomlinson, Junior Seau, or Ben Coats. The reason that I will to is because I wasn't given the gift to be, they were. I asked the question again, what did you do to deserve to be so gifted? They looked at me with a piercing stare waiting for me to give the answer because obviously they thought it was a rhetorical question. I asked for answers and each of them said the same thing ... I did nothing.

Wow, you mean to tell me that you are this gifted and you did nothing to get it? You didn't even ask for it? You just woke up one day and discovered that your gifted? Yes and that is the very reason why you need to be humble, appreciative and acknowledge that you did nothing to earn the gift, He just decided to give it, because it comes without repentance and He won't take it back, but if you don't use it then you've missed your purpose.

When I was done speaking to the team, man I was on top of the mountain. God had blessed me with a message that was on time for those that were present. I left there with my peacock feathers on display, I mean, I was walking in my purpose and my calling. I had made a declaration that I was here and that I was gifted and the gift made room for me. You are a creation of the creator and the creator made no mistake. Make a declaration today and walk though customs ready to walk in your place of Purpose.

The next level in your process is presenting your items to the customs officer. You may have taken something with you, like fruit or tobacco for example, which may not be permitted in your place of destiny. What do you do, if you have brought something along with you that is not permitted where your destiny is? Do you not go because you so desperately think you can't live without them … no you leave them at the border and you move ahead. I don't care how much they cost, what sentimental value they have, how long they or it has been apart of your life, there comes a time when you have to realize that where you're going you cannot take everyone with you … you have to let some people go. Now this is not saying that they a bad people, no not at all. It simply suggest that they are not the right people.

Let me see if I can express it in the fashion. Sometimes there may be two wonderful people in a relationship but over time the relationship breaks down and they decide to part ways. Does that mean that they are bad people, no but what it does suggest is that they were not the right person for the place of destiny. You cannot feel bad, ashamed or discontent when you have to move on from those you came with. I was given a revelation about this when I had a layover while on a Delta flight to Houston. We flew out of Fort Lauderdale International and the plane was full. I met a few people while waiting to board as well as those who were seated near and next to me. Many times what happens is people ask me about my 2001 National Championship Ring from the University of Miami. We beat up on Nebraska, sorry Nebraska. Anyhow I am asked about it and then one thing leads to another in and before you know it they know all about me and me them. When the flight arrived in Atlanta, every one that I had met deplaned while I stayed seated because the layover was 45 min. While waiting it hit me like a ton of bricks. My revelation that day was, there are many people that start out with you on your way to your destination. You enjoy having them there but the reality is they are only purposed to go with you as a part of your journey. They leave your life and go to fulfill their purpose else where but they served their purpose while with you. You can't cry about them leaving, you can't get upset about why they had to go, all you have to do is sit patient and wait. Yes wait because when your life is on a layover the best thing for you to do is wait. Why wait? Why not try to stop those who are getting off? Why not try to even go with them? Well you can't because your ticket is for another place. Don't get confused thinking that where they are going is your destiny neither get offended when they have to walk out of your life … you need to let them go, why you ask? Well the answer is while your waiting, you have an opportunity to relax. To assess your travel schedule and prepare for the destination. Your flight may have been delayed or even detoured so you may have to make adjustments but what you have to recognize is that while your waiting, someone else is waiting on you. They are at the gate waiting to get on with you and ride with you all the way to your destiny. The blessing in it all is that the people who I met on the layover I still have relationship to this day. They have been a source of inspiration for me, but what if I became closed off and upset and didn't want to speak to them because of those that started out with me left me? You got it, you would have missed an opportunity to be in the moment while being Passport Ready. When you are Passport Ready you don't long for what was, you live in what is utilizing your gifts for your future.

People will come and people will go, you just have to decide how you are going to respond when they have to leave. Some will leave thinking they hurt you by their absence in your life, some will leave because their destiny is different and their purpose was fulfilled but you are the only constant in it all and you have to know the difference … its ok to let them go and its ok to leave others behind. What you lose in the fire you will find in the ashes!

Chapter Six

New Expectations …
(I refuse to go back)

If you are always trying to be normal you will never know how amazing you can be.

Dr. Maya Angelou

What amazing insight by Dr. Angelou. Trying to be normal is the same as being ordinary. To be normal is to conform to a type, standard or regular pattern. It means to not deviate from that norm. It is to have average intelligence, simply put it means that you stay where you are the way you are because you're convinced that's all you are. However, I am here to tell you that you are more than what you see. I love the writing of the Apostle Paul. Paul tells us over and over again that we are better than are failures and our faults. Paul says in Ephesian 2:10, "For we are His workmanship created in Christ Jesus for good works (a clause). We are His workmanship, another translation phrases it as we are His masterpiece … I like that, I am a masterpiece. A work of outstanding artistry. You are greater than a Picasso, Rembrant, or a Michelangelo. As great as these artist's paintings were they too were created as a master piece, this is why their works are priceless perfections of artistry As I stated in the previous chapter you are gifted and God didn't make a mistake when He supplied you with the gift. It may have taken a little time for you to discover your gift but that's apart of the process, but what you can't do is keep things status qou once being awaken and inspired.

What you cannot do is go back to your way of thinking. Every year on the last day of the year, most evangelical Christians like to have what's commonly known as watch night service. This service is designed for the adherents to bring in the new year with God. We say a familiar world wide phrase in our churches as well as in the clubs when the ball drops and the new year is ushered in … Happy New Year, but has the year changed or transformed you just because it's a new year or are you still thinking the same way as you did the year prior? Might I suggest to you that as time moves forward you may be stuck in time. I say this because if you have gone into a new year with the same mindset as the previous year, there's nothing New or Happy about the current year. Please understand that if you change your way of thinking, believing and trusting then you can experience something greater for your life. If the mind is willing the body will follow. If you keep looking back you never will advance ahead. Its so elementary but there are countless of individuals with this mindset, they have gravitated toward this way of thinking. You've been wearing the same hairstyle for 5 years, visiting the same restaurant and ordering the same food items. You haven't challenged yourself to change, you have just normalized your life. Some would say that they are content. But contentment doesn't mean that you are satisfied. It means that you are ok with where are but not who you are.

It is time for you to evolve into the person you where purposed to be and that is the True You. Yes the person that you must discover, the reason why you were born, that true you.

The realization and the new found knowledge of self has giving you the ability to accept the truth about you and cause you to celebrate your weaknesses and embraced your flaws. You are the true you that no longer marches to the beat of someone else's drum but have become your own drummer and band leader. You are not afraid to walk alone because you know who you are and you know that your validation is not in the people around you but in the God that created you. You have found the true, and it was only achieved by refusing to go back to the false you that everybody loved but you hated. Welcome to destiny and purpose, but let me warn you, there is danger ahead if you start to look back.

Looking back prompts you to desire going back. It may have been successful back there, but where you are headed what's back there doesn't fit for the future. Many churches that are dying are trying to recapture the glory day of old. They have not done anything different in the past 30 years and they are hanging and holding on to tradition. Tradition has its place, however tradition is nothing more than frozen success.

Many people have a great infatuation with past success. Don't get me wrong your achievements are great resume influencers, however, if you continue to live back there and not evolve in your field and perfect your craft then the world will pass you by. A great example of this is the University of Miami football program. While working at the U we had experienced great success. Five national championships, 48 First Round draft picks since 1984, 40 Bowl appearances, 20 National Award winners including two Heisman Trophy Winners, 77 All -Americans, the most consecutive years with at least one player drafted in the first round in NFL draft history (14yrs) and 7 NFL Hall of Fame inductees. As you can see we were a really successful program, but a shift happened and we were unaware of it taking place. We got comfortable with what we had done that we didn't see how other school were thinking. They, the likes of Alabama, Clemson and others began to steal away from us those elite athletes to their programs. We thought that because of our past success player would always want to be apart of a winning program, however what else did we have to offer other than our past success? The paradigm had shifted and we got caught sleeping ... settling with success. These other schools started upgrading their facilities and building new buildings with everything that a talented student athlete would want. On the other hand all we did was build a new weight room and put in new turf. We tried to catch up but we were too far behind and the effects of that decision, to rest on our laurels caused us to experience major defeat. We went through a decade of good season but not great. We were the team to beat of every team we played they wanted to kick our you know what, and they did. What happened to us? For years on end we held the longest home winning streak but now we were losers. I attribute our decline to being settled with past success. While we were living in the past, other programs where making progress and we lost the recruiting battle because we lacked the facilities to attract highly gifted athletes. We did so much with so little for so long that we thought it would always be that way, but we were sadly mistaken, we had become a has been, but thank God for visionaries and velvet purses that have helped the U to return to relevancy. The administration hired a great athletic director in Black James and then one of the most successful College coaches in NCAA football history in the personality of Mark Richt. New facilities are being erected one in particular is an indoor practice field to help with rain storms that would hinder practice and make it nearly impossible to get quality work in.

What is the lesson from this example? If you rest on past success without mining for more meaningful goals then you are on the pathway to failure.

However, there is good news, because if failure occurs you must know that it is not final. Failure is not final when you shift your pain through process and then find your passion then eventually your purpose. When going through valley moments, you can't look back but must continue to move forward with hope in your heart. What then is hope?

Hope … Ernest expectation. Hope is not wishful thinking. Many believe in wishes thinking that they have hope, however, when we have authentic hope we patiently wait for what we are expecting even when it may be painful. In the book of Romans, Paul speaks of such a thing when he references Abraham. In it he details,

Rom 4:18

Who against hope believed in hope, that he might become the father of many nations, according to that which was spoken, So shall thy seed be.

Listen to the beauty of this language from the King James rendering, who against hope believed in hope … that's powerful. Having every reason not to remain hopeful, Abraham stay expecting. Hope seemed against him because of his current condition, but he believed in hope (in God), that what he was waiting for would take place. He had been introduced to a God that he never knew but is now communicating with him. Angels have made a visit to his home, all he as to do is believe in hope.

Rom 4:20-21

He staggered not at the promise of God through unbelief; but was strong in faith, giving glory to God;

And being fully persuaded that, what he had promised, he was able also to perform.

A beautiful portrait of trust and patient. He staggered not. This gives a picture of one who has lost their trust and now is wavering as they go along this journey. It gives a vivid picture of a person under the influence of an intoxicant and has lost the normal facilities of the body and sensory has been diminished. They can't assess situations well and their vision is impaired. They are trying to walk toward their destiny but they don't have the three essential elements to make it, Faith, Trust and Hope.

Faith is your ability to trust what you believe, trust is your firm belief, it is unshakable and hope is that level of expectation that eagerly awaits the fulfilment of your faith. Abraham possessed these three qualities but they had to be developed, it was a process of a decade of perseverance, but he staggered not!

Where is your faith? How would you describe it? Does your faith carry you and do you trust what you believe? God has gifted you with an incredible amount of grace and giftedness. Set your expectation of you higher and believe you will get to where you see yourself being. Don't just dream about it, rather do those things that are necessary for you to excel and exceed, whatever your spirit directs you to do … do it!

One day you'll wake up and one day you'll see, that fiction become fantasy and fantasy become reality and you're not in a dream. It's a path we all must take and a path we all must make, although there are narrow and misspoken ways but it's a path we all must take. You've got to go up or down there is no other way around. So fulfil your dream, make it reality. Fulfill your dream it's your fantasy don't get trapped in just dreaming. Life is a dream but nothing comes to sleepers but a dream. Stay Awake.

Chapter Seven

Living Life Intentionally
(Purpose, Planning, Prosperity)

What does it mean to live life intentionally? It means that you wake up each day with a great expectation to be better than the day before. It means you are purposeful in your actions and you speak life into each day. It means you live a life that is meaningful and fulfilling to you. It means you make thoughtful choices in your life. Being intentional means you actively interact and engage with your life. Intentional living is a lifestyle and not just a goal.

Each day is planned, even if you plan to do nothing but relax to reassess where you are and make plans to prosper. Lets take a look at one of those powerful verses from the Word of God found in the Books of Poetry ... Psalms 1.

The Way of the Righteous and the Wicked

[1]Blessed is the man[1]
    who [a]walks not in [b]the counsel of the wicked,
nor stands in [c]the way of sinners,
    nor [d]sits in [e]the seat of [f]scoffers;

[2]but his [g]delight is in the law[2] of the LORD,
  and on his [h]law he meditates day and night.
[3]He is like [i]a tree
  planted by [j]streams of water
that yields its fruit in its season,
  and its [k]leaf does not wither.
[l]In all that he does, he prospers.
[4]The wicked are not so,
  but are like [m]chaff that the wind drives away.
[5]Therefore the wicked [n]will not stand in the judgment,
  nor sinners in [o]the congregation of the righteous;
[6]for the LORD [p]knows [q]the way of the righteous,
  but the way of the wicked will perish.

What I like most about the Bible and other sacred text, is that it is such a practical literary work. If you look through its pages you will see many precepts for practical living. Notice here in Psalm 1, the psalmist admonishes the reader on what it means to be blessed. Firstly, he says that when you live life intentionally you do not take counsel from the ungodly, what does this mean? Well, it describes a method of seeking those with wisdom and righteousness. Those who will not give you direction that is antithetical to your purpose and destiny. It informs you to examine those who you associate with that their lives have been that of integrity and morally alert. This does not connote a person that is perfect for none of us are, rather it is expressing those who have a relationship with the creator and have made good decisions and their lives reflect that. You have to surround yourself with those who will help you and not harm you. Secondly, you live life intentionally when you refuse to be engaged into activity that is illegal and morally inappropriate. Jesus said that a tree is known by the fruit it bears. Don't allow your circumstances to provoke you to stand with those that will give you advise for a quick fix, that will profit you in the immediacy but will entrap you to continue this particular behavior. I have made decisions in my life that I still feel the affects of today. You don't want to have regrets in your life ... they haunt you until the day you depart. Thirdly, the seat of the scornful. It is said that hurt people hurt people. I'm sure you can think of someone that has something to say about everything and everyone. The are distasteful, disrespectful, disdainful, mocking and mean. If you spend time with people like this their attitude can and will affect you. They are a cancer to your purpose and destiny. You soon will become as they are. If you allow that kind of character to enter into your spirit you will forfeit your dreams and destiny.

This one verse illustrates to us the progression of digression. The swift way of decline. Notice, the text moves from Walking to Standing to Sitting. The intentional perspective is to move upward not downward, to move forward and not backwards. When you finally focus on you, you will be able to see others more clearly because your focus is inward. You know the areas where you need to adjust and get fixed in your life. You have cleaned out the clutter of familiar faces and voices that didn't challenge you to be great. Yes, I challenge you to step out of your comfort zone and seek higher ground, not higher ground of safety but a summit of success. You have to elevate your expectations while climbing the slippery slopes of the mountain, the jagged edges underneath your feet. In spite of all of the challenges you have to believe. I have this saying, I can be slowed down but I cannot be stopped. I expect to win and my perspective on losing is that I win even when I take an L, I learn and I grow from each life challenge. I am intentional and purposeful in addressing my failures. I have come to know that failure is not final.

You deserve the abundant life. Jesus spoke of His coming as the conduit to abundant living. Now this life is not about wealth and fame according to (Boice)

· Abundant life isn't an especially long life
· Abundant life isn't an easy, comfortable life
· Abundant life is a life of satisfaction and contentment in Jesus

Contentment comes when you have found your purpose. The thing God has prepared for you. It is a place of being unsatisfied with who you are but ok in the moment of where your are. Speak life over yourself with positive affirmations and live in faith as though you have made it into your purposed place.

Now the difference between contentment and satisfaction is a beautiful emotion called Happiness. One of the synonyms for happiness is well being. Many individuals put so much of who they are in others. Again, you cannot give the responsibility for your happiness to someone else, that is unfair to them and an unrealistic expectation. Let me attempt to frame it this way. If you are not happy in your relationship you need to focus on you and not your spouse or your partner. You need to reassess why you selected them and reflect on your choices. Realize that you chose this person to be in your life for several reason and reevaluate your decision making methods. Did you pray? Did you choose them to fulfill a void in your life? Did you use them to help bring a sense of stability to you as a person or did you make a decision based on your profession? What ever the answer is you need to know that if you placed in their hands your happiness, it was an unfair expectation and responsibility to give that to them. Now you have not found your happiness and you have burden them with your baggage and transferred it to them whereby creating dysfunction and disappointment. Now you have hurt, harmed and hindered your life and progress and have set them back and possibly caused them more pain than you ever anticipated, all because you didn't have a sense of happiness and wholeness when you invited them into your life. What is needed to be stressed is that, no one is responsible for your happiness but you. You have to be content and satisfied with you based on where you see yourself and not how others may perceive you. Do not set your expectations up this way, rather work on your goals internally and externally. Ask yourself the hard questions and ask others advise on how you may do things better or on how you affect their lives. Get feedback so you can make those adjustments inwardly and become a whole person rather than a splintered individual who seeks happiness in others. Secondly, look around your life and the relationships you've been in. Investigate how the people who have been apart of your life have benefited from your being there. Are they collateral damage or are they benefactors of a value added individual. Remember as I stated in chapter three that some people are in our lives only for a season. We think that it will last for ever but the truth is some are seasonal but still can have a life long affect. Have you been a blessing to others? Reflect on your past and know what you have to leave in the past as well as what you need to take with you into your future. Life lessons are mined from the hardest places in our lives but the most beneficial in our development and growth … this is prosperity and I am happy!

> "Happiness is not something ready-made. It comes from your own actions."

> — Dalai Lama XIV

Chapter Eight

All Inclusive Life
(I Paid the Price)

Life is such a journey that we seldom take time to embrace moments of meaningful development. For many the constant uphill climb has left you exhausted or even overwhelmed. The expectations that you have placed in others have left you with more questions of your value and purpose coupled with the disappointment of not providing for yourself the care you need. You have gone through a lot and now you only want to be at peace in your life. Yes, you desire the struggle to be over and what you are going through you want it to be through. One of the things we fail to realize is that the struggle has a purpose. It has given you a greater appreciation for life and the fulfillment of your purpose. Yes you paid the price to be you! You say to people that comment about your life that they wish they had what you have. Truly you tell them that your life comes with a warning label … It Cost to be Me! Every tear you've cried has a coded message in it. Every pain you felt has made you better. Every form of resistance has made you stronger but it all came at a premium price. Its time for you to live your All Inclusive Life!

When I speak of the all inclusive life, I am suggesting that life is synonymously paralleled to an all-inclusive premium resort. These are the resorts that you have paid a major price for, that will provide you with amenities that are not found at less expensive all-inclusive resorts. There is a psychology to the all inclusive option. Researchers have discovered that there are serval factors why people want to be at an all inclusive resort.

Professor of economics and psychology at Carnegie Mellon University in Pittsburgh George Loewenstein, USA suggests that any satisfaction, regardless of previous preconceptions, will do much to raise appreciation levels for value for money. According to Dr Loewenstein, those questioned in a study about whether they preferred concepts such all-inclusive holidays, where a one-off payment was required to cover all costs, many said they did "because then they could relax and enjoy the vacation more knowing it was paid up". This interesting insight into the psychology behind our relationship with the idea of the all-inclusive holiday shows that all people really want is a stress-free time on their vacation. If standards meet or exceed expectations, people are generally extremely satisfied with the experience and will likely to repeat it in the future (Faye Leonard holiday hyper market the benefits of going-all-inclusive 2015). The key phrase here is Paid Up ... everything that you will enjoy has already been paid for. You don't have the stress of continuing to pay and monitoring the expenditure or dealing with the psychological trauma of continuing to pull out our wallet, but you have paid for everything in your past that you can now enjoy your present. This interesting insight into the psychology behind our relationship with the idea of the all-inclusive holiday shows that all people really want is a stress-free time on their vacation. If standards meet or exceed expectations, people are generally extremely satisfied with the experience and will likely to repeat it in the future (Leonard 2015). You deserve to have moments where you have no stress. You deserve moments where you can be taken care of after taking care of so many others. You have paid a price for what you are enjoying now.

Look at the process. You paid in your past for what you will enjoy in your future. What you didn't know was the payment method. Your time of preparation for the moment of pleasure. You submitted to the renovation process and didn't settle for remodeling.

In the renovation process things had to be torn down, taken out, pull up and plucked out. What this process did was create more capacity in you rather than a simple remodeling. You upgrade your life by submitting to the process of perfection, remodeling is a rearranging of the same furniture or even the purchase of new pieces, but the problem is your dimensions haven't change ... you are till the same. However, those who have been renovated have paid a price and when the job is complete what a wonderful experience it is to see a vision come to fruition. Its time to pick your fruit. So go ahead and order that steak and lobster ... its already paid for. The Don Perignon that you have been waiting to taste is waiting for you. You don't have to worry about paying again because you paid in advance for the enjoyment if the present. Give yourself permission to be taken care of. Stress free living. Your mind needs it!

From a psychological perspective, all-inclusive resorts are aimed at specific demographics, says Elliott Jaffa, a behavioral and marketing psychologist:

The Lazy Traveler. They want everything at their fingertips and don't want to have to look outside of the resort for excursions.

Recreation Lover. These users want a lot of recreation opportunities on-site so they don't have to leave the resort to enjoy themselves.

Sequestered & Satisfied. The alcohol may be watered down in the drinks, but at least they can get them anywhere they want.

Scared Safe. There's a safety factor when going to South or Central America, and the chances of getting mugged are lower at a resort.

Consider all of these factor and ask yourself, what is it that you desire and deserve. For me its all four. I give myself permission to be lazy just for me. I want to enjoy myself in life where I don't need to go far away from me to enjoy me. I want opportunities in life that will afford me the enjoyment of selective surroundings without the worry of worry. I give myself permission to be free and safe. I release myself from the perception of people and only dance to the beat of my drum. I give myself permission to not have to look over my shoulder for those who have spoken confident words to me to only to turn on me. I give myself permission to look beyond them knowing that everyone you count you can't count on and every one that's with you is not for you. I give myself permission protect me in spite of what other think. I have paid the price for my all-inclusive and I will enjoy it because I deserve it.

Chapter Nine

Living My Best Life
(From Promise to Fulfillment)

Hip Hop artist Lil Duval has a song that has become so popular because of one stanza … I'm Living my best life. Many within that culture have take that line to mean that their lives are full of happiness and joy. Filled with accomplishments and achievements. They have a sense of financial independence (relatively speaking) and their lives are in the best place that they have ever experienced to this point in their lives. I say relatively speaking because living your best life has levels to it. What I want to suggest is that living your best life is living a wonderful experience that you've never have had in your life. You may be reading this book right now and sailing the seas for the first time and saying to yourself, "Life doesn't get any better than this." Its relative to your experiences and no one can tell you that your best life experience isn't the best because you are having this experience and not them. Lets look a bit deeper into this philosophy of Living your Best Life.

"I'm livin' my best life / Made a couple Ms with my best friends / Turned all my Ls into lessons."

So starts Chance the Rapper's intro to Cardi B's 2018 track "Best Life." A couple of months earlier, Wiz Khalifa dropped a single also carrying that name. And last month, UK rapper Hardy Caprio did the same. On Instagram, the #liveyourbestlife hashtag has clocked more than 865,000 posts and counting. HuffPost has an entire section dedicated to the idea. "Live Your Best Life" graced the cover of a September 2005 book comprising the best articles from O, The Oprah Magazine. A quick Google search of the phrase, meanwhile, delivers 6.1 billion results, including articles, books, social media accounts, and websites dedicated to helping you do just that (Heather Snowden *Highsnobiety* 2018).

Dr. Rebecca Turnbull says that living your best life is living the life you love and loving the life you live. What I didact from her philosophy is the best life is your life … not you parent or your spouse but yours. You don't compare others living to yours. To some working out before the sunrise and juicing it up is the best life, however, you may work out at noon and have your smoothie doesn't mean that because your not the 5:00am riser that your life is not best for you. You cannot live your best comparing subjectively your life to someone else's. It is said that if you love what you do then you will never work a day in your life. The meaning is its not considered work to you but to the person next to you that doesn't love it they see it as laborious and wish they could be far away from there. The most important word in this phrase is "your." It is imperative that you continually examine your life. Far too long in my life I have strove to make the life of others happy. Family, Faith community and friends alike, but I have come to discover that I became fragmented in the process. Don't get me wrong, I know my life is a life of service, however; the constant pursuit of doing for others left me feeling unappreciated. It came to the point where helping others was hurting me, I wasn't living my best life although I convinced myself that I was. The expectations that I allowed to be placed on me from a faith community nearly caused me to fulfill an act of self-annihilation. People want to impose on you their perceptions of who you should be because of the title you have and the position you hold. A family, spouse, sisters, nieces and nephews taking your heart and generosity as a right and not a privilege, thereby taken for granted the blessings given. The major idea here is that if you are trying to live your best life through people then you may be setting yourself up for major disappointment.

What I declared to do to live my best life was to consider me first. If I am not the most important person in my life then I can't be the person I need to be for those I love. I am a person that loves to help others and it does bring a smile to my face and warth to my heart, but now I want to live my best life so, I need to do those things that make me happy, content and satisfied with who I am and what I have become and want to continue to grow to have a greater impact.

If you want to live your best life its time for you to take some chances. Go back to school, start that business, leave an unfulfilling relationship with people that suck the energy out of you and never help to replenish you. Enter into a relationship where you know this person understands you and will not get in the way of you being you but will help you achieve. Surround yourself with people that bring out the best in you. Now the caveat here is bring out the best in you and not just the person that says they want the best for you, there is a difference. I have been in relationships with people that tell me they only want what's best for me, but they were determining what that was, I was a vision facilitator but not a vision caster for my own life ... don't make this mistake! Its time for you to simply say no to the things and the people that you've been saying yes to for far too long. Its time for you to lean on what God has placed in you and to stop depending on others to validate what you want to do ... you don't need their permission to live your best life.

> "Today if anything is trying to hold you back, give no attention to it. Get your hopes up, get your faith up, look up, and get ready to rise up."
>
> — Germany Kent

Conclusion

Thank you for taking this journey with me. When I got the inspiration to write this book I was filled with so much doubt and apprehension. I listen to the negative voice rather than seeing myself as an already accomplished author and this book as a best seller. What I have come to realize is that it doesn't matter how many copies of this book are sold, what matters is the one person this book helps to look at themselves and their world differently. I hope that through these pages you have discovered the true you or are on your way to finding that person. I hope that you have develop a sense of self and have declared that your validation is nowhere but in the hands of your creator.

I hope that you have become Passport Ready by shifting your expectations from others on to yourself. I want you to come to a place of self-actualization and self-realization. You have the capacity now to do it … whatever it is. You are a value add individual. The most important person in the world is You! It has to be because if your are not the best you or a better version then you can't be the best you to those who you serve and are a blessing to. Remember to stay in touch with you. Don't settle for where you are but continue to strive for more. Make plans and fulfill your goals. Don't rest on past success rather build on it.

The journey is not over but it is just beginning because you have your passport in hand and now you are ready to experience life at its best. Not by any one else's standard but your own. You are fee to see the world and as you go remember there is someone waiting for your arrival. You are the asset and not the liability. You are above and not beneath, you are blessed and favored, you are moving and no longer stagnant, you are Passport Ready!

Author Description

Steven J. Caldwell is inspirational, encouraging, a motivator, an achiever and an over comer. Having over come the streets of Chicago's south-side, drug addiction and homelessness in Miami to becoming a successful professor, pastor, team chaplain and trans-formative life coach makes him one that knows what it takes to shift your paradigm and elevate your expectations to a level where you see beyond what you can see and sense. He has worked with countless of NFL stars from their college careers as team Chaplain at the University of Miami. Men such as Ed Reed, Andre Johnson, Vince Wilfork, William Joseph, Reggie Wayne, Santana Moss David Enjoku, Duke Johnson, Jimmy Graham and many more. He has been a source of counseling and encouragement to those who have experience great lose. When Chicago Bears great Walter Payton passed, Steve help his son Jarred to properly grieve and turn his tragedy into triumph, winning the MVP of the 2004 Orange Bowl against Florida State. Steve was voted as the most inspirational professor at Florida Memorial University where he teaches philosophy and world religious perspective. Professor Caldwell is a value added man and is able and capable to lift your life to a level where you can move and make those necessary changes to make you Passport Ready.